SMART LEADERSHIP

Leadership Explained in Simple English

THOMAS JOHN GRALAK

DEDICATIONS

This book is a personal gift to all the people who had encouraged me to write this book. I dedicate this book to my students, friends, and other authors who gave me the power and inspiration to make it. I'm being thankful to my prudence for giving me the opportunity to meet new people who became my friends, as the editor of this book, Mehmood Rehman (Reymani Mmr) who put his heart into my book and helped me in making my dream come through and true. I would like to express my warm feelings to my dear family, the most important part of my life. My mum, sister, and brother who are the foundation of who I am and the spiritual inspiration of what I'm doing.

At the end of these short but very honest and deep dedications, I want to thank you. Thank you for holding this book in your hands. We are like sisters and brothers who share the same passions and interests. Thank you for giving me the possibility to create this special communication with you.

COPYRIGHTS

Smart Leadership by Thomas John Gralak © 2020
The right of Thomas John Gralak to be identified as author of this work Effective Businesses and Effective Leaderships has been asserted by him in accordance with section 77 and 78 of the Copyright, Designs and Patents Act 1988. All rights reserved. No part of this publication may be reproduced, stored in a retrieval system, or transmitted in any form or by any means, electronic, mechanical, photocopying, recording, or otherwise, without the prior permission of the author.

Any person who commits any unauthorised act in relation to this publication may be liable to criminal prosecution and civil claims for damages.

ACKNOWLEDGEMENTS

Writing this part is the most stressful. Honestly, I am so lost in searching for things, people, life events, and the very spiritual meaning of existence itself. That being said, how can I not thank and plainly forget everyone who shaped me into who I am and what I do? Yes, it is such a difficult task to include everyone that made the water ripple but the most complex tasks also give the most satisfaction.

Therefore, let me recognize the ones who provided me the courage in talking to you about something that I do for a living, something that has changed my life and how it can change and shape your life for the better. Here it goes. To all the people I have hurt in my life, the ones I could not ask forgiveness in person but I want to through this work of mine. To my father who I forgive now as he made me stronger by all the troubles he had levied on my feeble shoulders, and I used boxing as my solace, so thanks to my boxing without which I would have detonated into millions of hurt crystals.

Most importantly to God, who has always been my guide in life and helped me in finding my true self, giving me the confidence and peace to live life as a gift. One of the gifts that he aided me is my family and friends. My educational career provided me with ample quality friends, friends who stood by my side and were true to their words. These friends were professors, lecturers, classmates, students and even the university staff members; all of them have added value to my life from time to time. Especially Tom, Nahara, and Damian; I will love you forever.

Last but definitely the most important people I would like to offer my sincere thanks to is my family which includes my mum, my brother, my sister and anyone else that added value in my life. Thank you everyone for being there for me, being the pillar of my life and supporting me emotionally. Thank you so much to all the people that stood by me when I was a silhouette. Without you all I would not have been able to compile my thoughts and experience into words.

TABLE OF CONTENTS

DEDICATIONS	2
Copyrights	3
ACKNOWLEDGEMENTS	4
INTRODUCTION	7
Companies and Leadership	11
Factors of Leadership	14
The Unheard Leadership	18
The Leadership Styles	22
Orientations in Leadership	25
The Spirit of Leadership	28
Emotional Intelligence is the New Leadership	31
Can Managers be Called Leaders?	35
Traditional Vs. Effective Recruitment	38
Motivation or Motivational Leadership?	42
Communication and Leadership: Same Message?	46
Why Leadership?	50
Companies Breathing Leadership	53
The Learnings of Leadership	64
References	75
Meet Thomas Gralak	84
Other Books by Thomas Gralak	86

INTRODUCTION

What comes to your mind when the word leadership passes through in front of your eyes? Is it someone higher in status, shouting at their staff and getting the job done? If your answer is "Yes", you need to rethink and reimagine the real definition of Leadership.

Leadership comes with many definitions and concepts. But all in all, it means one thing: The Art of Managing People to Create Maximum Output. Now, as shiny as it seems, this is often not the case when we imagine leadership around us; especially in businesses. Leadership has changed dramatically and the aware organisations are taking benefit from their adoption while the centralized or rigid organisations fail to keep up and adapt to this new wave of smart leadership.

This new leadership is no longer one-sided. It does not have alpha-male personalities dictating each single-step or else you're fired rules. Instead, this new leadership is in its true essence a soothing concept that treats a staff as part of a team. No longer is the staff called staff, they are recognised as a team. Their voices and ideas are heard and just like a closely knitted family, the modern leadership has a set of job families and their leaders are captains who appreciate their sailors at all times.

Leadership nowadays is concerned with various approaches regarding the management of businesses as affectively as possible. Modern businesses have to be aware of all the related issues to choose leaders that fit in the best possible ways with the everchanging characteristics of organisations. And for that reason, it is crucial to understand what actually leadership style does. According to Business News Daily (2015), "There are many distinct leadership styles that have evolved over the last 80 years of study, each embodying a different set of traits and skills.

Yet for all of them, one fact holds: An effective, successful leader is one who has the ability to inspire". The early leadership style research had been first conducted in 1939 by a group of scientists driven by psychologist, Kurt Lewin (Business News Daily. 2015).

From that research, it can be seen that leadership style has evolved over the last decade, and therefore, it is essential to be mindful of the existence of different leadership styles. Within many different organisations, doing different kinds of businesses, current and future effective business performance is directly related with the way the company manages its people.

Also, among various leadership approaches, possibilities to adopt and to constantly changing business environments is not just a key to compete as affectively as possible, but it is also crucial to survive within the extremely competitive market. According to McDermott et al (2013), "There is no one best leadership style. Effective leaders may need more than one style in their repertoire. Good leaders adapt their behaviours, signals, and commitments in line with strategic goals in order to convey appropriate and realistic expectations to their employees".

How many times in your life have you had to face an extremely uncomfortable situation related to your professional life? We have to rely on other people who are in charge of public services, such as government institutions, schools, police, National Health Service and so on. Why the service they provide is often ineffective and leads us, the customers to frustration? According to Parliamentary and Health Service Ombudsman (2015), "Almost two in three people who are unhappy with a public service don't actually make a complaint and 29% of those say they believe that complaining will not make a difference".

Now, the same issues can be encountered within places we work in. We experience things such as lack of understanding, unequal treatment, discrimination and lack of possibilities to share ideas. The environment of our professional life is full of unprofessional leadership approaches, and has a colossal impact on our job performance, creativity, wellbeing and so on. According to Independent (2015) who carried out research among British workers, "Data collected by Investec Private Banking found that 25 per cent of professionals, including those working in finance, law, teaching and healthcare, are unhappy with their work-life balance".

Nevertheless, to be effective as a society and professionals, we have to rely on knowledgeable people who are aware of modern business solutions necessary to build wellness; creating a sense of security and justice. But where should our main focus be? It should be on issues related to modern leadership, and what managers can do to improve productivity and business performances within many different sizes and types of business.

Are there many successful companies managing in a very effective way like I mentioned? Yes. The effective ways by which a company manages its workers has a massive impact on business performance. The most important component of every organisation is its motivated and highly satisfied workforce. If these traits are present in any company, regardless of their size, it those organisations will reach to a successful leadership model. How are companies doing that? Let's find out.

COMPANIES AND LEADERSHIP

All the big companies you see around you like Google, Facebook, Tesla, Microsoft, and the list goes on and on; these companies are above others for a reason. It is not just their money which keeps them above their competition. Then what is it? Most of the successful and effectively managed companies are gigantic and powerful because they are aware how important is the notion of effective leadership. According to Feser et al. (2014), "Telling CEOs these days that leadership drives performance is a bit like saying that oxygen is necessary to breathe. Over 90 percent of CEOs are already planning to increase investment in leadership development because they see it as the single most important human-capital issue their organizations face returns".

There has been a considerable interest in the impact of effectiveness for the leadership styles on business performance. According to Chief Executive (2015), "Today's companies need effective leaders at every level and in every location. To deliver on results, CEOs can't do it on their own. They need more fully performing leaders than ever before".

Companies have found the way to make themselves as affective as possible within a very demanding market when it comes to leadership. So, they can become a role model for other companies to achieve strong business performance in order to compete as a key player. Therefore, the question that needs to be answered is what other, less effective businesses can do for their leadership, motivation and communication to create a sustainable competitive advantage.

Previous researchers, like Kurt Lewin, had conducted research which discovered three different leadership styles. And in the coming years, there has been considerable interest in research concerned with leadership. New generation of scientists such as Kendra Cherry Cameron Boykins, Gary Yukl have explored forecasted information related to different leadership approaches so as to define all the new styles that have evolved over time. This notion is further explored by the new research about leadership. It provides substantial knowledge necessary to understand the most effective leadership styles which are essential to perform any business effectively. So, what questions need to be answered?

- **What is the most effective leadership style?**
- **What are the main factors that impact effective business performance throughout all the leadership styles?**

Besides these questions, there are many factors when it comes to leadership as this concept is not new. Leadership has been around us since the first human on Earth. So, there must be a lot of factors that contribute to this concept. What are those factors? Let's uncover them one by one.

FACTORS OF LEADERSHIP

All the factors we will see into are related with the usual Human Resource Management (HRM) concept. These factors circle around this model and then add all the neighbouring areas which can define in detail the essence of an effective leadership. The main factors such as the recruitment processes, communication levels and motivational notions have to be searched in detail to find the current and the relevant information about the effective leadership performance.

To find what less successful organisations can adopt in their leadership styles to improve their business performances, they should have a checklist of the following objectives:

- To find the most effective leadership styles.

- To analyse successful and influential organisations and find their leadership approaches.

- To study the modern business solutions relating to the leadership styles which managers can use to boost productivity and streamline their business performances.

- To summarise information about leadership, effective recruitment, motivation and communication to help design the most effective ways in finding the relevant people to perform the leadership roles efficiently.

According to Business Case Studies (2015), "Leadership is the art or process of influencing people to perform assigned tasks willingly, efficiently and effectively. Enabling people to feel they have a say in how they do something results in higher levels of job satisfaction and productivity".

So, effectiveness concerned with leadership within any modern business is a crucial step all businesses need to perform above or at par.

The importance of effective leadership has evolved many decades ago. The research conducted in 1939 still provides an explanation concerned with how leaders really operate. One of the most successful researchers in this area was Kurt Lewin, a German psychologist who provided the theory saying that the way humans behave should be seen from their everyday lives and how they interact with other individuals. (About education. 2015). Now, according to Cherry (2010), Kurt Lewin's research established three basic types of leadership styles:

Authoritarian: This kind of leader provides people with clear information about what and when it must be done. There is a strong borderline between the follower and the leader. In this particular model of leadership, leaders mainly make decisions singlehandedly without any consultation with their team. This kind of leadership approach has a colossal impact on decision quality, which is low because other peoples' creativity is completely ignored.
Participative or Democratic: In this particular model of leadership, it talks about the leaders who cooperate with their team in order to work out the best viable solution. Lewin found that the authoritarian-led group was more productive. But surprisingly, the output of democratic-led group was more qualitative. The research clearly shows democratic leadership style as more efficient.
Laissez Faire: These leaders leave all decision-making processes left at the hands of their team, and they offer little or no guidance. In most cases, Laissez Faire was ineffective because people were not equipped with any important details necessary to create the high-quality productivity. But this particular kind of leadership can be very effective in a team with higher qualifications.

Another research conducted by Kurt Lewin provided some new insights for managing people. Leadership is mainly concerned with creating an effective business environment where cooperation between individuals has to be performed in the best possible manner. So, an authoritarian approach can also be useful in places like army or prison where others' point of view does not matter.

How about Laissez Faire? In case of modern businesses, it would be extremely ineffective because without any bright leadership; it is impossible to create a responsive business environment.

Democratic approach is strongly associated with effective leadership because cooperation between individuals plays an important role in creating a high-performance business environment. So, only one style described above gives out a strong foundation for understanding and creating the best definition for an effective leadership.

There are a lot of approaches in the market as entrepreneurs and scholars are uncovering the concepts behind the true leaderships and how certain approaches can help them. Besides the ones we talked about above, there are a lot of other approaches which are rarely talked about. Such approaches need to be surfaced for an effective understanding of the true meaning of leadership; a thing we have been focusing on for some time now.

So, have you heard about these unheard approaches? If not, let me guide you through them.

THE UNHEARD LEADERSHIP

As we find more and more about the levels of leaderships and the cultures of different organisations, our leadership methods and approaches will keep changing. But there are some approaches and changes which need to stay with the concept of leadership. This is essential for a smooth functioning of the organisation processes and the overall management structure fluidity.

Recent studies have revealed existence of new leadership styles, which are mostly effective within modern businesses. According to Cameron and Boykins at al. (2013), in the contemporary market, an awareness of five leadership styles is essential for managing a project successfully.

- Command & Control Leadership: This kind of leadership is very effective in cases where the team is more familiar with what is necessary to do in order to achieve the right business goals, but needs a leader to provide them with the necessary guidance in case of any urgent obstacles while in the process. This leadership style is most effective in a situation of crisis when teams are not fully aware or knowledgeable about any particular task. People within the organisation who have little knowledge about the goals need a leader who is able to provide clear guidelines and direction towards that goal (Meyers 2012).

- Relations-Oriented Leadership: That strong ability to encourage people to bond with each other can best be described as a relations-oriented leadership. This kind of leadership plays a very pivotal role in creating a highly cooperative team to attain the proposed business goals. Also, people want to be a part of this kind of business environment because their opinions and the way they act within the team are important to others and to the leader (Morely, 2013).

- Hands-On Leadership. This kind of leadership is able to completely assume the role of leadership. The ability involves cooperating together with employees to complete with the company goals. Also, the internal communication within the company is crucial to get the feedback from their staff in order to maintain a highly motivated team.

The external communication is essential to gather the customer feedback so as to respond adaptively to a changing environment (Travis, 2013).

- Coaching leadership. Leaders of this kind are mainly focused on the development of their workers. Coaching leadership develops people for the future to create a highly knowledgeable team. Coaching style is very effective in order to boost team morale which also helps in building up competence and confidence of individuals (Benincasa, 2012).

- Democratic Leadership. This leadership style is an effective way to engage all the team members into the decision-making process. In this model of leadership, to effectively communicate within work environment and to transfer the ideas between staff members; an effective communication is essential to utilize. The knowledge related to open communication in the case of democratic leadership will be an important business tool which is necessary to use to create highly motivated teams and a responsive business environment. (MindTools. 2013).

A research conducted by Cameron and Boykins have provided a new understanding of the effective leadership styles. Most of the styles described above have evolved from Lewin's democratic approach based on successful relationships between individuals, which are essential in the modern business world. The command and control leadership style, defined by Cameron and Boykins does not fit into the modern definition of leadership as it is only linked with managing day-to-day activities which is a task for managers, and not for leaders. Effective leadership is when it is linked with the leading people for the future.

So far, we have looked into the different leadership approaches and a lot of times, many entrepreneurs fail to study about such approaches and end up making the wrong decisions. Lack of application for these approaches creates issues in leadership styles as well. What sort of issues? Let's get into that…

THE LEADERSHIP STYLES

This one is super important. And it is linked with the approaches which means it is a dependent variable on the type of approaches being used in leadership and eventually, this shapes up the leadership styles which the leaders should incorporate in their daily operations and processes. There are many leadership styles to choose from as this department has been researched on by psychological factors as well.

Psychologists and researchers have added enough data on this topic to write books on books. But we will be looking into the way the approaches affect the overall leadership styles. These styles can make or break organisational cultures. Are there steps being taken to ensure the styles are compliant to the culture of the organisation or up to par with the market demands?

During the past half century, a number of studies have examined different leadership behaviours. According to Yukl (2012), "In most of the early research on leadership behaviour the focus was on describing how leaders influence subordinates and internal activities in the work unit". Yukl's research provides a new insight about the leadership performance which is crucial in knowing the most effective approaches. According to Yukl (2012), there are four most effective leadership styles:

- Task-oriented
- Relations-oriented
- Change-oriented
- External

The task-oriented leadership is the usual milestone or goal-setting leadership which provides a task. This task should be completed on time and without any inefficiencies. The relation-oriented is a leadership style which promotes interpersonal communication rather than the task assigning we saw above. Leaders and the team are correlated and are working in harmonious relationship-building environment.

The change-oriented leadership is always in favour of changing environments and being adaptive to all the challenges thrown at it. This leadership is AGILE and this is a very good move for organisations which like to update its processes and challenge the status quo.

Lastly, the external leadership is when there is an outside help to the team if they are unable to complete the job successfully. Much like the task assignment but instead of just assigning task and checking back when done, this leadership ensures the job is completed even if requires additional help from external sources. We have briefly touched on these four styles. Let's look them up in more detail.

ORIENTATIONS IN LEADERSHIP

These styles are also known as orientations as orientation is a way of doing things and that is exactly what these styles show. Let's check the styles we briefly described above in further detail.

- Task-Oriented Leadership: This kind of leadership is focused on resources such as people, equipment and so on which are utilised in the most effective ways in order to get the job done (Yukl, 2012).

Task oriented leaders within this managerial performance mainly concentrate on:

- Planning concerned with the clearly assigned tasks including identifying essential action steps.
- Monitoring.
- Clarifying concerned people with crystal clear guidelines to ensure that the team is provided with the best possible knowledge to accomplish the tasks.
- Effective problem-solving approach. In case of any problem, manager provides their team with the necessary support.

- Relations-Oriented Behaviour means creating strong relationships with the team to create the best possible outcomes. This kind of leadership is mainly focused on:
- Supporting others to create a friendly work place environment in order to build cooperative relationship.
- Developing the concerned people and providing them the valuable career advice and supporting employees to improve their skills.
- Recognition involved with appreciation of the team.
- Empowering concerned people by creating opportunities for others to share their ideas in order to make final decisions.

- Change-Oriented Leadership can be described as having strong possibilities in changing internal and external business environments.

There are distinct approaches concerned with this particular leadership style:

- Advocating Change approach can be seen in a situation when there is no obvious crisis. The certain skills to analyse current situations provide the businesses a great advantage to avoid any disturbance and prepare the company for any unexpected events.
- Envisioning Change approach described as an effective way for the leaders to engage in new initiatives and strategies.
- Encouraging Innovation is concerned with inspiring others to become more open-minded and creative in terms of business activity.
- Facilitating Collective Learning leaders to build effective work environment which is based on innovative approach, internal activities can be used as a motivational tool in order to create new ideas and learn new knowledge.

External Leadership Style is concerned with providing the information within internal environment about external events necessary to boost business performance.

- Responding includes lobbing for assistance and resource, defending and promoting the excellent reputation of the team.
- Networking is essential for leaders to maintain and build relationship with superiors, peers and outsiders who can provide valuable business information.
- External Monitoring is concerned with the analysing of business threats and opportunities within the unpredictable external business environment. It is critical to introduce necessary changes in order to form strong and competitive business.

All these amazing additions to the leadership approaches and the leadership styles will strengthen the effective leadership model. But just like any vessel to a body, the soul needs to be fulfilled in order to attain peace at all levels. Likewise, for leadership to be effective, its spirit should also be in tune with the levels, styles and approaches we have talked about above. What is the spirit of leadership? Let's find out in the next chapter.

THE SPIRIT OF LEADERSHIP

This leadership style is unique. Why? Because this is the core of all the leadership approaches, styles and all the previously discussed concepts. Such a leadership is truly the spirit as it defines the entire body of leadership which we visualise within our organisations and businesses.

Recent studies have provided new essential knowledge necessary to understand a spirit of effective leadership. None of the approaches examined should be described as a leadership style. For example, task-oriented approach is related to managers, who control people within the organisation in order to finish a certain project. An effective, modern leader paints the bright future related to any business activity. A leader is someone who can form a strong sensation of trust; necessary to create high performance business environment.

Previous researches have revealed many diverse leadership styles. It can be seen that the new findings about leadership have evolved and moved towards teamwork-oriented style which can be described as democratic approach. In the today's business world, it is essential to cooperate effectively within the company in order to build a strong business environment, which is able to exchange information within the organisation and with its external surroundings. Also, highly knowledgably leaders have to know how to form a highly motivated workforce to cope with extremely challenging business reality.

According to Ghasabeh et al. (2015), "The business environment is constantly changing as organizations are increasingly participating in global markets. Globalized markets place demands on the roles of leaders in organizations operating in this modern environment".

Adaptive Leadership

Unpredictable business environment needs people who are able to adapt themselves to unexpected changes. According to Fraser (2015), transformational style is concerned with possibilities to combine number of different learning approaches in order to achieve best possible outcome in the changing business environment. Transformational style is also called Adaptive Leadership style.

Are You an Adaptive Leader
Source: Forbes

The table above shows the adaptive leadership styles which are crucial within an unpredictable and constantly changing business environment. One of headings is emotional intelligence which is vital in maintaining highly effective, motivated and a responsive staff.

What differentiates a soul from robots? Emotions. So, if there is a spiritual leadership style or an approach, will there be emotions associated with the leadership? Let us uncover that mystery by studying the importance of emotional intelligence in effective leadership.

EMOTIONAL INTELLIGENCE IS THE NEW LEADERSHIP

Emotional Intelligence is a new topic for many researchers. It is not as old as the concept of leadership. So, it does not have much research done to it. But over the last decades, the progress on this concept is phenomenal. Why? Because of the importance it brings for not only leadership by the overall concept of businesses and organisations. Emotionally intelligent organisations are ruling the market nowadays and this topic has been receiving the most attention is research and development to study the factors which can be implemented in organisations for its success.

Recently many researchers made attempts to define Emotional Intelligence. According to Suan, S. et al. (2015), it can be described as the "capacity to perceive, understand, integrate and manage one's own and other people's feelings and emotions, and to act upon them in a reflective and rational manner".

Palmer and Stough (2001) added that the emotional intelligence of leaders is extremely important in managing organisations. The ability to deal with people in a professional manner is super essential. One should know by now that emotional intelligence is an extremely important component for an effective leadership style. According to a research conducted by Suan et al. (2015), "performance of the organisation is directly related to emotional intelligence of its leaders".

A deep knowledge about all the different ways of dealing with different types of people is essential in achieving a high-performance business. A sensation of trust, understanding and a good relationship between the team members can only be created by leaders who possess a sturdy emotional intelligence.

Emotional intelligence plays an extremely important role as a component of a leader's personality. Adaptive leadership style is directly linked with emotional intelligence, and in other words one cannot exist without another. To form a successful business environment, emotional intelligence is a critical factor in order to cooperate with staff in the most effective way.

To cooperate effectively within challenging business environment, awareness of different leadership styles as well as possibilities to apply the most relevant ones depending on situations has to be fully accepted by any modern organisation in order to perform successfully, both in terms of the team and their customers.

According to Baesu and Bejinaru (2015), "Nowadays leaders must be more adaptable in this context of continuous change and uncertainty. Future leaders will have to adapt their leadership style depending on the context, ensuring that results are obtained". This research clearly shows the two different leadership styles which are directly related to Emotional Intelligence:

- Transactional leadership can be described as the approach when the leader performs as a manager of change, attaining important transformation with the team so to improve productivity. In others words, this certain type of leadership is linked with traditional approach and is more relevant to managers than leaders.

- Transformational leadership is a style of the leadership which empowers subordinates to reach the organisation vision, in order to increase productivity and employee motivation, create successful workplace as well as enhance professional and personal development of the workforce.

Transactional vs Transformational

Transactional Leadership	Transformational Leadership
Leadership is responsive and its basic orientation is dealing with present issues	Leadership is proactive and forms new expectations in followers
Works within the organizational culture	Works to change the organizational culture by implementing new ideas

Source: Slide Share

The table above shows two different leadership styles. A transactional leadership represents more traditional approach which describes task-oriented managers. But a transformational leadership clearly represents modern and more sophisticated method deeply concerned with emotional intelligence. There is a colossal difference between the two approaches which has huge impact on the overall business performance.

In other words, the transactional approach is a less effective method as it concerns managers with limited knowledge. Moreover, managers are focused on certain tasks related to business activity. They do not think about the future and the way they deal with their team is less effective. On the other hand, democratic leadership approach has evolved over the last century and appears to be the most appropriate style. As transformational leadership is strongly linked with the democratic approach, it shows the new ways of dealing with challenging modern business world.

Also, transformational leadership is strongly concerned with emotional intelligence which is essential to work out the best possible ways to cooperate with others in the most effective manners. A deep understanding about these possible ways of managing people supported by emotional intelligence is one of the many critical factors in creating a powerful leadership performance.

A lot of people are double-minded on leaders and managers. Emotional intelligence can be infused into any individual but only a true leader knows how to use it in the right amounts and at the right places. But is a manager worthy enough to be called a leader? Let's discuss some forms of leaderships to compare the types of leaderships and if managers can be called **LEADERS** or pioneers of **EFFECTIVE LEADERSHIP.**

CAN MANAGERS BE CALLED LEADERS?

Most of the recent studies state that managers can be also leaders. This statement is completely wrong and does not make much sense in today's business world. It is essential to understand that managers differ from leaders. Managers can be described as people who are task-oriented; they just want to get things done. Therefore, modern managers often apply authoritarian approach which could be effective in places like army, where soldiers have to follow orders without asking any questions. Can the very same approach be used for all departments or in this case humans? No. Because in the business world where human creativeness is essential, authoritarian approach is not effective at all.

In modern business world, the importance of effective leadership is priceless. The new generation of leaders has to be able to create a sense of hope, trust, compassion and stability. These four factors are deeply concerned with emotional intelligence which is crucial in order to create effective business environment. Moreover, to respond to this changing business environment, people within the company have to follow their leader in order to achieve a common goal. Therefore, strong skills of influencing people is an inseparable factor of success. An effective leadership is involved with heading towards the future.

Transitional leadership is mainly concerned with managing people in order to get certain tasks done. And it should change its name from 'transitional leadership' to 'transnational leadership'. On the other hand, transformational leadership is concerned with influencing people towards a common vision. A trust is an essential factor to ensure people will follow you. To create a sensation of trust among staff, leaders have to love their job and people they work with.

Nevertheless, to find the best candidate for leadership, effective recruitment process is an essential. Communication and motivation are some business tools necessary to utilise in the best possible ways to form a successful business environment. In an effective recruitment process, there are three essential factors necessary to identify perfect candidates for a leadership position.

The first one is knowledge of the most effective leadership styles which is essential to perform business activities. Also, it is vital for the best candidate to present an understanding of motivation and communication techniques in a constantly changing business environment to create the required responsive and an effective leadership performance.

Also, it is vital for the best candidate to present an understanding of motivation and communication techniques in a constantly changing business environment to create the required responsive and an effective leadership performance. Modern businesses should be aware of the process for selecting the most relevant people to perform certain leadership jobs. As it has been previously mentioned, a constantly changing environment has a huge impact on business performance.

According to Kurt Lewin, the business organisation can be described as an unpredictable environment which is characterised by an unplanned self-organisation. Therefore, it is crucial for modern organisations to be able to adapt to constantly changing business environments. According to Lewin and Minton (1986), "If organizations are complex systems, management and change take on a new dimension".

It can be seen that an unpredictable business environment impacting any modern business has to be managed by people who are aware of a wide range of difficulties that they may encounter in everyday life, especially with regards to the challenging and extremely competitive market. So, a clear understanding of current global business situation, makes it possible to apply the most suitable leadership style and profound business knowledge related to the ways people have to be guided is of utmost important when it comes to creating a successful business performance.

One of the easiest platforms to assess leadership levels of an organisation and the leadership qualities an employee brings to the company is the recruitment stage. But, just like traditional leadership, traditional recruitment too needs to be reformed. How? To do that, we would need to first compare and contrast.

TRADITIONAL VS. EFFECTIVE RECRUITMENT

What's wrong with the traditional recruitment? Many things. As the pandemic hit the world, recruitment processes were in chaos as organisations were losing a lot of their employees rapidly. But in order to hire new talent, where did they go to? Traditional Recruitment methods? No, they introduced new ways of recruitment and adopted all the technological mediums they once neglected. That practice has saved them millions in their budgeting and planning and now organisations are using online mediums or modern recruitment methods to find the right people for the right job, and the people who are willing to do the job.

The importance of effective recruitment and selection process for an effective leader has a massive impact on business performance. According to Chron (2016), background-based interview is an effective way to select best possible candidate for the position of a leader. It can be seen that the previous work experience is one of the most important criteria during recruitment process. In some cases, it can be an effective way to find a candidate for the other jobs. But what other traits are we looking for in that candidate besides their availability? Passion, sacrifice, dedication and emotional intelligence are value additions which we need along with to find best candidate for a leadership position.

The traditional recruitment process is mainly focused on candidate competencies, which currently seems to be an effective way of selection. A number of leading companies, which have changed their recruitment process from competencies-based interviews to strength-based interviews have started to evolve this concept and it is being endorsed by other organisations as well. To select the best possible candidates, brands such as EY, Barclays, Nestle and Royal Mail utilise strengths-based interviews. The strength-based interviews differ from the traditional ones. Comptences such as experience, educational background are not as important to perform a certain job. The strengths of a candidate are essential to boost the productivity within an organisation. How to find that out? By using strengths-based interviews. They are perfect in finding out the candidates who are fascinated about their future tasks related to their professional job.

According to University of Kent (2016), "Competencies are behaviours that an organisation needs. Competency-based interviews have been the most common type of graduate recruitment interview for a long time. Competencies can be defined as what you CAN do, while strengths are what you really ENJOY doing".

In the case of candidates for leadership positions, it is crucial to possess certain skills such as emotional intelligence and be adaptive to a constantly changing environment. Also, a strong desire to develop an understanding about leadership is crucial to boost productivity and create a responsive business environment within the company.

Within the new generation, market effectiveness is a key to powerful business. Business effectiveness is important in every aspect of business activity such as communication, motivation, strategy and the recruitment process. As usual, the recruitment process is the first stage of entering a new company. Therefore, the process of selecting candidates has to be extremely effective in order to find the best possible candidates.

According to the current business trends involved in the recruitment process, the strength-based interviews can be described as powerful business tools necessary to be used in the modern-day businesses. Managers have to operate within the changing environment full of unexpected events, which is extremely stressful. Therefore, hiring people who can enjoy challenging work for being a leader is crucial to build an effective business. Unfortunately, most companies on the market apply competency-based interviews which cannot effectively evaluate candidates; therefore, their productivity is not as effective as it should be. To avoid implications and make best possible choices, strength-based interview can be the best solution.

Because of the lack of research related to best possible recruitment processes, there is certain uncertainty about which approach is the best. It can be seen that a strength-based approach has been adapted by many leading brands which have resulted in improvement of productivity (Crush at al. 2014). Besides the approaches, competences of potential candidates are also important in the effective selection processes.

Besides recruitment, employees are creating job families instead of segregated workforces. But this new practice of leadership and its components raises a question on the motivational aspect of the employees. By adopting effective leadership, is it sufficient to be motivating or is there a need to bring in motivational leadership?

MOTIVATION OR MOTIVATIONAL LEADERSHIP?

Motivation, just like its counterpart, has been around for some time now. From Hawthorne studies and beyond, it is the first thing asked in interview questions and practised and focused on by public speakers, entrepreneurs, employers and even managers. So far, the issues related to leadership styles, effective ways of selecting relevant managers, challenging constantly environment and managerial adaptation skills have been discussed. But to build an extremely effective business environment through leadership, it is essential to be aware of the importance of motivation.

Motivation in modern companies can be an effective tool in building effective business performance. Current generation of business owners and managers along with the different transformational leaders have to apply various tools of motivation. According to Chron (2015), unmotivated employees within the company have a negative impact on turnover rates and productivity. So, the importance of motivation is priceless and can help to explain the ways of how to effectively boost people productivity in order to achieve excellent business performance in the various businesses in the market.

To most of us, motivation is concerned with rewards which can effectively create a strong desire to work among other team members. It may have been the best reward in the old times but it is no longer the case now. Recent studies clearly show that 'trust' is one of the most important components for an effective motivation. To motivate people in a certain company, trust is essential. Therefore, the main question is, how to create that feeling of trust which is an extremely important factor to form a sustainable and responsive business environment within a company.

The most important factor necessary to create trust has already been discussed in the previous sections of transformational leadership. This style has a huge impact on staff motivation and is linked with emotional intelligence, which is very important in dealing with people in the best possible manner. Such a way of managing staff can by described by words like understanding, supporting, coaching and developing.

Also, an effective transformational leadership performance is concerned with strong adaptation skills which are crucial within the constantly changing environment. According to Bass (1985), "Transformational leaders are known to empower followers and consider their individual needs".

Therefore, understanding and empathy plays an important role in motivation. "As a result, leaders' behaviours, such as intellectual stimulation and individualized consideration, represent a kind of social exchange resource for expressing respect and consideration" (Basu & Green, 1997). Emotional intelligence can be seen as an inseparable factor concerned with the sole concept of motivation. To create a strong motivation drive, it is essential for leaders to be constantly in touch with people within their organisation.

To communicate effectively with the new ideas, strategies, any changes related to business activity leadership which can perform speeches, and are the most effective ways of communication. Also written communication can be utilised to boost staff productivity. But it is not as effective in motivating people as verbal communication (Zhu and Akhtar, 2015).

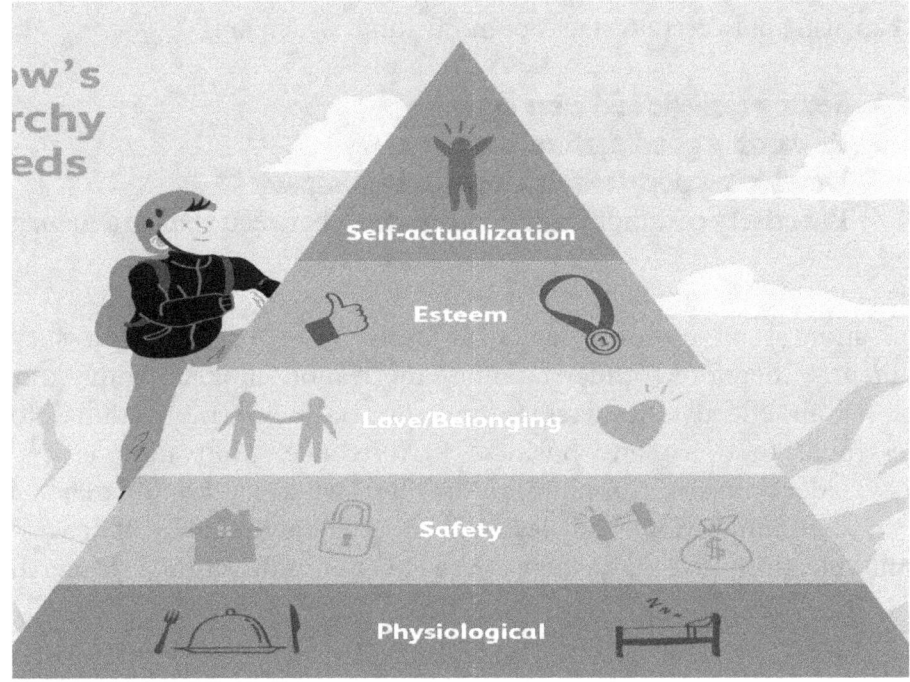

Source: VeryWell Mind

The diagram above presents Maslow's Hierarchy of Needs which is a very important concept about the overall intrinsic and extrinsic motivation. According to Forbes, "It is a psychological theory saying that we need to have certain basic needs like survival and safety fulfilled before we can work on higher needs like love and belonging, self-esteem, and eventually achieving our full potential".

Awareness of Maslow's Hierarchy of Needs is essential for managers to understand what forces drive staff to be more effective. All the levels shown in the pyramid in modern world can be achieved throughout the professional walks of life. All the levels of life motivate people so managers can utilise the concepts from Maslow's Hierarchy and create an effective motivation system.

According to Leadership-central.com, an extrinsic motivation can be described as an effective business tool which leaders can utilise to boost team productivity. This type of motivation is concerned with the physical rewards such as bonuses, gifts and different types of activities.

Moreover, according to Allegheny College (2015), to motivate teams, leaders can also apply certain stages of motivation, which are:

1. **Setting realistic and clear goals.**
2. **Rewarding good performance.**
3. **Developing positive thinking within company.**
4. **Effectively communicating information between staff and management.**

Motivation is an essential factor to create an effective business environment. Therefore, understanding motivation linked with knowledge of an effective leadership, human needs and motivational tools is essential to boost any business performance. Motivation is a part of its older cousin: Communication. But what is the difference between communication and leadership? Are there any differences in communication just like there were in the motivational leadership?

COMMUNICATION AND LEADERSHIP: SAME MESSAGE?

Communication is the process of making sure the message sent has been received and a feedback is received back. But in the leadership process, how to make sure the feedback is calculated in its original terms? Or does the concept of communication need a remodeling of its structure?

Nowadays, it is essential to be aware of the importance of communication. According to Boyle et al. (2014), "communication is a multidimensional skill that constitutes different aspects, and therefore, a comprehensive approach is required for a better understanding of the same. As a subjective matter of the study, it is a major challenge to validate the vast pool of material".

The information above provides basic understanding of the importance communication plays in any leadership activity. It can be described as a multidimensional skill, which within the modern business, is a dire step needed to perform a business activity effectively.

Also, internal communication within the company as well as the external communication is crucial for a business to interact with existing and potential customers in order to collect information which is essential in the creation of a desirable product or a service. So, an effective modern model of communication is necessary which can be first understood and then applied at all the selected levels. That is not all, the value of communicational understanding in the present-day business world is crucial for leaders (Boyle et al. 2014).

And to create a high-quality communication within any company, it is essential to apply a modern leadership approach and the proper expertise in the field of communication. According to Johnson et al. (2014), four factors have to be applied to create an effective communication strategy for the team.

- Focus: Communication has to be related to the key issues involved in business activities. Also, information has to be clear and focused in order to enable all receivers into easily understanding the main message. It is also essential to avoid complex language and pointless information so as to create a highly understandable and an easy-to-follow message.

- Media: Information has to be delivered to the team in the most effective way, so a choice about the selection of the best possible mediums to convey information within the company will have a significant impact on the final performance. Take for example face-to-face meeting, it is an effective way to deliver information but this kind of communication is extremely difficult to apply in any established company, isn't it? What to do then?

Well, conferences and workshops seem to be a great solution for this, because managers can reach to a bigger number of the team. If a company is hiring a large pool of employees, other communication solutions have to be applied. Modern technology provides solutions such as company newsletters, video conferences, voicemails, blogs and so many other mediums for an effective communication.

- Employee engagement: Even if the communication is focused and is provided to the team via an effective media, it would not be enough to create an effective communication. People within the company have to create a strong community first which shares the same values and objectives. If a company meets the requirements described above, it will never be a problem to encourage the team in following the new strategy concerned with business activity. Also, managers can use motivation to speed up the process of employee engagement. For example, Births, a public-sector organisation organises meetings with their team members after introducing a new business strategy. During the meeting, the team has to promise that they will follow the new strategy.

- Impact: Communication has to be powerful and impactful in order to make the necessary changes within the company. To achieve expected level of impact, the message has to be made in strong and memorable words.

There are two main goals that have to be achieved by communication within an organisation. The first goal of communication is in keeping all the people in the company as updated as possible. The second equally important one is concerned with communication being able to create a well-connected community within a company (Simons and Ridder, 2004).

The studies related to an effective leadership which can be seen above clearly show that an effective leadership have to possess a unique set of personal skills such as compassion, emotional intelligence, respect and passion. To effectively perform leadership roles, the person driven by passion can only be inspired by others to create a common vision. Certain business tools such as communication and motivation have to be disrupted in order to form a business environment full of innovative people who are ready to share their ideas. By such addition, this new generation of leaders have to be knowledgeable in the area of research and findings concerned with the most effective ways which can be used to boost productivity.

Therefore, knowledge related to best possible leadership styles, certain business tools such as communication or motivation and the most effective way of recruiting people is essential to apply for the new leaders' generation. We have talked in great depths about the types of leaderships, approaches, the direct and the indirect factors that affect the whole concept of leadership. Now, you might be thinking about the reasons why leadership needs to be updated, right? Why is it necessary now than ever before? Let's discuss that…

WHY LEADERSHIP?

We have found out a lot about leadership even though this topic is not alien to any of us. Still, the major researches being in this science should be of concern to all of us. It shows how important this concept is and how seriously we should take it to apply it in our daily organisational lives. We will talk about the reason as to why do we need to research on leadership. We can do so by using all the ways to evaluate the new findings in the field of leadership, recruitment process, motivation and communication methods.

The notion of finding in-depth leadership research findings can be explained by the dire need to find out what less successful organisations can do in terms of their leadership style to improve their business performance, taking into consideration the exploration of different companies applying various leadership styles, researching impacts they might have on the performance and how recruitment processes, communication and leadership can influence the business infrastructure.

To analyse in detail a current situation associated with effective leadership, a case study approach is the most effective way in order to analyse the topic in the best possible way. A deep scrutiny of leadership is essential in order to discover the modern biasness issues (Yin, 2014). The case study research approach is the most effective in the case of the topic concerned with this work because it enables detailed examination of the business as an organisation, the person as a manager and the group as a team. A capacity to create a clear image from this intensive research leads to an effective conclusion which is essential to build new theory (Sounders et al. 2009).

In the case of effective leadership and factors such as the recruitment process, motivation and communication in a particular time played an important role in order to perform high quality research (Sounders et al. 2009). Because the leadership concept is constantly changing, a cross-sectional research approach within this work provides us an effective way of analysing case studies related to the variety of different companies at a certain time, which are found to be an essential conclusion, necessary to build final theories about leadership.

Okay, so to provide you the examples from the big companies practising leadership, let's uncover the secrets of some of the biggest names you might come across in this age. One of them was a market leader which lost its position for not updating leadership styles and methods in their organisation.

COMPANIES BREATHING LEADERSHIP

Facebook

The importance of leadership and how it influences any company can be seen in the case of one of the most influential companies in the world: Facebook. According to Forbes, Facebook is ranked as world's tenth most valuable brand. In the near future, Facebook might tremendously improve their rank within a very competitive environment. The companies such as Apple, Microsoft, Google, Coca-Cola, IBM, McDonald's, Samsung, Toyota, and General Electric have been ranked higher than Facebook.

Amidst the all-time players active in the market, Facebook has recorded the highest growth. The one-year value change has been 54%. Comparing this data with the Apple, the company which is ranked in the top tier, they have recorded 26% of one-year value change. This data clearly shows that Facebook has a huge business potential. But higher potentials lead to major questions. The question is: What kind of factors have contributed to Facebook's success? David Livermore has interviewed Bill McLawhon, one of the Facebook's top managers. The conversation between them was mainly related to an effective leadership approach. The Facebook top manager claims that the ability to inspire and influence people is the key to perform effectively in business.

According to Livermore, "Leadership is not conferred based upon your position and title at Facebook. It comes naturally to individuals who have a high level of impact. Who are the individuals who create extraordinary value quickly? That kind of impact leads to followership, which confers leadership. The people who 'ship it' and make an impact are the ones who are going to emerge as leaders". The top Facebook leaders also reveal that the managers they are looking for have to demonstrate two things; impact and character. So, these can become the two kinds of personality traits demanded by one of the most powerful companies in the world. Livermore also confirms five leadership abilities created by Facebook's founder, Mark Zuckerberg, which are important in forming an effective business environment. These leadership abilities are as follows:

- **Encourages Ownership:** This is concerned with smooth operations. If someone identifies any problem which is caused by someone else, there is no point to make a noise about it; the point is to efficiently remove the problem.

- **Inspires Others:** Trust in team within Facebook is crucial to build independent thinking. To enable people to unleash their creativity, Facebook tries to create a friendly and effective workplace rather than the usual bureaucratic obstacles.

- **Does Real Work:** Even the founder of Facebook Mark Zuckerberg still makes sales calls. It shows that even if you are a top manager, you still have to do the job which benefits the company.

- **Speaks and Rewards Truth:** Communication is the key to form a successful business. Throughout effective communication, teams can be provided with feedback related to their work to generate a better performance in the future.

- **Treats People with Extraordinary Respect:** To respect others is essential to create an effective business condition. Appropriate attitude and behaviour within the work place can have a colossal impact on team performance. So, the way you treat and speak to people must be full of respect.

The monumental business success of Facebook is based upon the modern leadership style. This new way of managing people is concerned with choices of the best leadership skills possible. A lot of business knowledge is equally important in order to create a high level of performance within the business environment.

A survey carried out by InnovationCoach.com asked questions associated with the factors impacting business performance. The answers given by half of the respondents were strongly related to 'inspiration' (Brands, 2010).

The success of Facebook has been achieved by bright leaders who are able to create responsive and friendly business environments. The way of leading people within Facebook is very innovative where leaders support their staff not just to accomplish certain tasks related to business activity. Effective leaders of Facebook act like a coach who can accept mistakes and mould them in the right way of doing the same things in the best forms. leader other young workers".

According to Business Insider, "Facebook has to scale, teach young people how to work for a living, and then teach those new, young workers how to work for a living, and then teach those new, young workers how to leader other young workers".

To create a responsive and an effective business environment, Mark Zuckerberg has developed innovative solutions in order to run an effective business model. According to Business Insider, effective solutions have been applied by Facebook. What were they?

- In order to boost productivity and apply effective communication, every new engineer receives six emails during their first day at a job. The welcome letter is the first one. The other five emails include information related to the tasks that need to be performed.

- To keep highly motivated team members, Mark Zuckerberg walks around his office every evening to talk to the people and help them if necessary.

- Facebook relies on small teams. According to Mark Zuckerberg, small teams made of three or five people can communicate very effectively between each other which results in a good performance.

- Every 1.5 years, team members of Facebook have to change their jobs. Engineers have to start working on a new project in order to improve their skills. This innovation has a massive impact on improvement in job specialization related to communication.

✓ Once a week, Mark Zuckerberg is fully available to their team to answer all questions related to Facebook activities.

✓ Facebook hires intelligent and creative people. To find the most suitable position for new people, it is essential to assess their strengths related to work-activity. Within this work-at-point, 2.3.1 effective recruitment process has been described as a key factor to be applied by leaders.

The examples provided above give clear understanding of solutions applied by Facebook in order to become as affective as possible.

Apple

A supreme example of one of the most effective leaders ever is Steve Jobs. He is an iconic founder of Apple which is one of the most recognised brands in the modern market. A huge success of Apple is based on some certain business solutions which were necessary to create an effective business performance which we have been talking about since some time now. The founder of Apple, who was also one of the greatest leaders of the recent decade, had this natural skill to inspire people and lead them towards a common goal (Brands. 2010).

According to Brands, inspiration can be described as "how people think, collaborate, and then put new ideas into motion".

This shows the utmost importance of collaboration which in other words can be described as communication. So, effective communication from top management and throughout the other company departments to factory floor and retail showroom is essential (Brands. 2010).

Behind an effective collaboration within the company lays inspiration. Inspiration can also be defined as motivation. Motivation is a driven force to boost creativeness and productivity which are important to create new ideas and improve the company's performance associated with its products and services (Brands. 2010). In the case of Apple, communication and motivation are extremely effective which can be clearly reflected in their financial results.

According to Apple Press Info (2016), "Fiscal 2015 was Apple's most successful year ever, with revenue growing 28% to nearly $234 billion. This continued success is the result of our commitment to making the best, most innovative products on earth, and it's a testament to the tremendous execution by our teams". Innovative business solutions are mainly associated with inspiration and collaboration which are essential drivers of creative business processes (Brands. 2010).

To effectively build powerful business performance linked with inspiration and collaboration, it is essential to take into consideration business factors such as:

- Innovation which within an organisation must be powered by an effective leader who is able to inspire people and implement changes for success.

- An effective leader has to set up clear goals.

- Enthusiasm within the company is a key factor in achieving goals of effective business performance.

- It is not enough to have motivational posters on the wall. It is essential to organise meetings in order to motivate people during the brainstorming which is essential to boost productivity and engagement.

- An evocative reward system is extremely important in order to improve the company's performance.

- Each business project has to be managed by effective leaders. Also, it is essential to measure the effectiveness of innovation associated with motivation and communication in order to introduce future improvements.

Two examples of Facebook and Apple shows the importance of certain features such as trust, understanding and flow of information which are strongly linked with the concept of an effective leadership. In the case of Facebook, which is one of the most effectively managed companies in the world, the importance of high performance within the business environment is essential. Moreover, the case of Apple clearly illustrates the importance of motivation and communication which are essential in modern leadership styles in order to form a responsive business environment.

Why is Apple practising such methods? It has done it to create an effective communication channel. According to Shaganaa (2014), in order to implement effective communication, Apple' solutions described below have been utilised:

- Online forum for employees has been created allowing them to share their concerns and ideas related to business activity. Also, members of the team are able to participate in surveys concerned with working conditions. The emerging solutions can help effectively address the problem and direct the effort into areas that need improvement.

- To keep a highly motivated team, stores within the entire supply chain are being randomly visited. It also helps maintain high standard of service.

- Apple provides financial aid for employees who need help. This solution has an influential and empathetic impact on enhancing internal communication. It also creates strong relationship between the team and the company which is crucial in order to fulfil staff expectations related to belonging needs presented in the Maslow's hierarchy of needs. This can be seen as effective motivational approach utilised by Apple.

- Communication with stakeholders is crucial in order to keep them updated and meet their requirements concerned with the product. To fulfil stakeholder's expectations, monthly meetings can be conducted.

In order to improve internal communication within Apple, every month a newsletter to staff is released. This solution is crucial to create strong well-informed work environment.

The solutions described and applied by Apple have helped to create effective communication, and improve team motivation levels.

Motivation within Apple plays a very important role. Apple has adopted a Maslow's hierarchy of needs in order to effectively motivate their team members. Maslow's hierarchy of needs has been previously discussed in chapter as a business tool that can be used by leaders to boost productivity. In the Maslow's model, there are five different levels of needs. The needs located at the bottom of pyramid are the most important for the staff Management of Apple Inc. (2015).

According to Management of Apple Inc. (2015), Apple provides their employees with average salary of $108,483 which is enough to provide them with an impression of safety related to physiological needs. Also, Apple gives to their workers a recognition bonus ranging from 3% to 5% of the salary. Moreover, Apple continuously is trying to improve health and safety standards in order to fulfil needs concerned with safety. According to Management of Apple Inc. (2015). "The Apple 2013 report illustrates the improvement in Apple research to provide employee a better workplace including support of social networks, work group and enhance worker-supervisor relationships".

The example of Apple presents importance of motivation necessary to be utilised by leaders to create a responsive business.

Nokia

Nokia as a company can be described as one of the biggest conglomerates which specialises in many types of industries such as electronics and power generation systems and power cable production (Nokia 2016). Over the last decade, Nokia had become a worldwide known mobile phone manufacturer. What happened later? Why had they lost a huge portion of the market share. When went wrong?

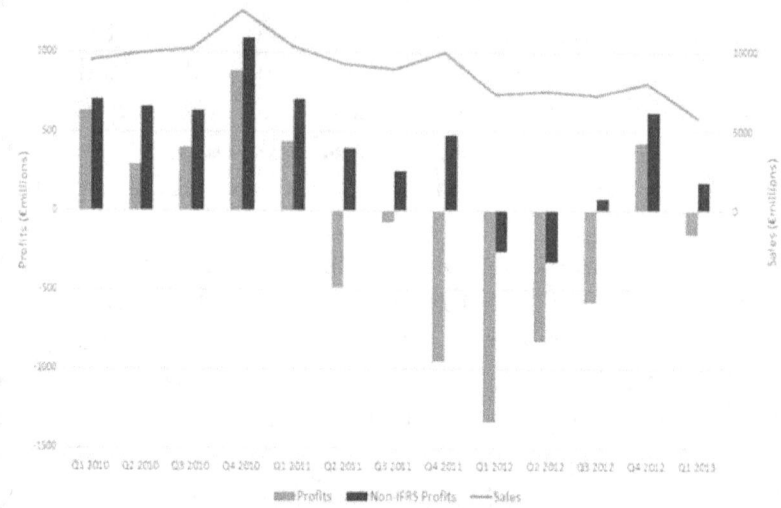

Source: All about Windows Phone

As it can be seen on the graph above, Nokia experienced a massive decrease in sales and profit after 2010. A pivotal company with a huge budget failed in keeping its profits intact.

According to the article created by Brahma and Mita (2015), four main reasons of Nokia failure have been pointed out. These reasons are as follows:

✓ **Software issues:** Nokia missed a business opportunity regarding its new software solutions. New trends associated with mobile applications were completely missed by Nokia which resulted in a massive drop of financial performance.

- **Customer issues:** Nokia used to be a customer-oriented company, so they were developing business activities and products effectively. At some point, Nokia lost its connection with their customers, and competitors such as Apple, Samsung, and Motorola took advantage of this lag as a great opportunity to reach their untapped new customers by meeting their updated expectations involved with mobile phones and mobile applications.

- **Organisational issues:** By entering the mobile business, Nokia showed excellent business performance. During certain periods of time, Nokia was developing new products desired by its customers. This development slowed down all of a sudden. Their business activity shot down and they lost all of their entrepreneurial potential.

- **Leadership issues:** Nokia used to be an extremely well-managed company. It experienced global success courtesy of an effective leadership style. Nokia used to be managed in the best possible ways because to become one of the most famous companies in the world, Nokia had to be proactive, risk-taking and innovative. Something happened in its organization. What was it? There are many speculations but no one is 100% sure how the market leader lost its rhythm in both its market share and market growth. As the fall became visible, it lost all of the competitive advantages and stepped aside its throne.

When Nokia became aware of their difficult business position; something had to be done. According to Brahma and Mita (2015), the CEO of Nokia, Stephen Elop decided to use communication as a business tool to solve the problem. To effectively reach all people within Nokia, he sent an email to all staff asking them about their opinion, for example: "How did we get to this point? Why did we fall behind when the world around us evolved?"

The information provided by Nokia's team gave an abundant amount of valuable feedback. Information provided by the team gave a clear understanding of the reasons which contributed to the dramatic decrease of Nokia performance. The information provided by Nokia's team gave an abundant amount of valuable feedback. Information provided by the team gave a clear understanding of the reasons which contributed to the dramatic decrease of Nokia performance.

Lack of internal communication in Nokia was one of the major problems. Because people could not communicate their concerns and ideas, the feeling of rejection was created among the team. Such a feeling had a massive impact resulting in the decrease in productivity. Also, external communication failed. Nokia stopped manufacturing products which were desirable by customers due to the lack of understanding for the current trends within the mobile industry.

In the case of Nokia, it can be seen that communication and motivation had a massive impact on general performance. Low motivated staff and a lack of communication were caused by ineffective leadership leading to unimaginable business consequences. Of all the leaderships we studied in these three companies, one thing is certain: Even leadership needs to be updated regularly. If Nokia had kept updating its processes and had spent on their research and development programs, it would still be a household name. Sadly, compared to the other two giants, Nokia lost its rhythm from the time it stopped focusing on the internal and the external leadership approaches and fell behind in the race of the market leadership.

However, Apple adopted the new leadership approaches and it is now a trillion-dollar company, a feat achieved by very few companies in the world. Likewise, Facebook too has diversified its leadership and kept experimenting by acquiring businesses, blending in different leaderships and introducing its effective leadership techniques to succeed in the market and still become the leader in social media platform services. So, in order for any company to survive, it has to design a well-planned leadership program to make the difference for the organisation and keep it above its competition.

THE LEARNINGS OF LEADERSHIP

Why effective leadership linked to business performance is so important? This question is critical to understand the factors directly impacting business performance within modern businesses and institutions. Apart from all the learning we have had so far, it should be clear that a well-executed leadership can launch any organisation to its successful path. The organisation size as we discussed before, is not the most important factor but the utilisation of effective leadership not at just the top management level but at all levels of the company.

Many different leadership styles have been described to find out the one which is the most effective. According to the studies on leadership carried out by leading researchers, the definition of the most effective leadership style is still not clear. For instance, some researchers such as Kurt Lewin, who was the first to attempt in identifying different leadership styles discovered 'autocratic leadership' approach which is completely incorrect, because the word 'autocratic' stands for a lack of trust, compassion, understanding and vision.

So, this particular approach can create sensations of rejection and add more pressure within the company. Withal, studies carried out currently regarding the leadership styles to some degree were also wrong because some of the styles discovered were directly related to this autocratic approach. It can be seen in the case of a command and control leadership style described by Cameron and Boykins et al. (2013). Another research carried out by Yukl (2012) described a style called task-oriented leadership which is also ludicrous because it refers to the autocratic style. So, being autocratic is mainly linked with a job of managers who are focused on specific tasks related to the business activity. To achieve business goals, managers control staff by giving them commands instead of supporting and inspiring them.

Leadership styles are not just definitions of certain approaches utilised by people who are responsible for managing the work of others within different businesses. According to the research that has been performed within this work, the most effective leadership style is associated with transactional leadership which can also be described in other words as an adaptive leadership style. The two styles that were mentioned above are mainly concerned with words such as understanding, compassion, trust and vision which are essential to create effective business environments.

Effective leadership style is not enough to create a successful business environment. Effectiveness of leaders is essential in order to react to the changing business environments, so as to boost productivity and form powerful business environments. Certain business tools have to be utilised by leaders to lead people in the best possible ways. The key to achieve good business performance is motivation and communication which is extremely important within the modern business.

Strong links between leadership styles, communication and motivation have not been mentioned by the researchers, so it is important to understand that concepts of communication and motivation are directly related to effective leadership practices. The business tools, one being communication is necessary to communicate with the staff in order to create strong relationship based on trust. Motivation can be described as a spirit or a drive force necessary to create strong business performance and encourage people to be as effective as possible.

The link between the most effective leadership style, communication and motivation is extremely important. In other words, it is possible to create a new leadership approach. The communication and motivation-based leadership approach can be the answer to the modern business regardless of the size or kind of business activity. A leader is someone who has the ability to cooperate with the people in the best possible manner. By 'best possible way', we do not just mean achieving certain goals of business activity, but much, much more. A communication and motivation-based leadership approach is able to inspire people towards the common future. The business environment created by this approach is full of compassion, trust and vision because to achieve highly responsive business environment; communication and motivation are both crucial aspects.

There is still one more factor concerned with effective leadership which is love. The examples of great leaders such as Steve Jobs and Mark Zuckerberg, who were presented earlier provide an understanding of success conglomerated with effective leadership. They became great leaders because they loved their jobs, so they were able to build some of the biggest companies in the world. Nevertheless, some people who are looking for jobs in order to become leaders within many different business areas have great experience and educational background which seems to be of a great importance.

Like old times, nowadays experience and education are not equally important anymore. To be an effective leader, attributes such as love, passion and devotion are essential. Now, to find the best possible candidates for positions of leadership nature, a potent recruitment process is critical. The recruitment process has to be designed to find people who will be able to love their job in order to create a successful business environment. The sad reality is that this critical factor concerned with recruitment process has not been identified by current researchers, so it is essential to apply strength-based recruitment processes to find the most suitable candidates for the leadership roles.

Leadership approach has a significant impact on business performance which has been proved by examples provided in this paper related to companies such as Apple and Facebook. These two companies are managed by extremely effective leaders who are aware of modern business solutions associated with motivation, communication and recruitment process. So, it is evident that innovative approach towards modern business solutions is essential in order to create responsive and powerful business.

An Effective leadership approach such as **C & M Based Leadership** can be utilised by small and medium size businesses as well. A false image of wanting innovative leaders to be used solely by big companies has been created. The example of Nokia clearly shows that even huge companies with a significant budget are very likely to fail in terms of business performance. Nokia used to be one of the biggest mobile phone manufactures in the world, nevertheless It lost its gigantic market share because of their innovative competitors.

Therefore, it is obvious that during certain time of Nokia's business activity, the effective leadership was not in place and out of tune. Lack of innovative approaches in terms of leadership, lack of communication and motivation within Nokia Corporation clearly illustrated that even large companies are exposed to considerable risks of business failure. According to Forbes, "8 out of 10 entrepreneurs who start businesses fail within the first 18 months. A whopping 80% crash and burn."

The information above provides the reality-check to the problems concerned with the current market, which is common for many companies failing to survive in the deep sea of competitor piranhas. To change this situation, modern companies have to take into consideration modern business solutions. Such kind of business solutions can be seen in the case of new leadership approaches which have been developed during the course of research conducted for this project. The solutions can be provided in the form of a new standard of managing personnel who are the most important resources within any business institution.

To boost productivity in the most effective way, the **Communication & Motivation-Based Leadership Approach(C&M-BLA)** could be utilized by businesses of any size so they can become sustainable and achieve an effective business performance. The Communication & Motivation Based Leadership Approach could be described as a real contender in terms of intelligent and effective ways of business solutions, which are necessary to apply in order to form excellent business conditions. Nevertheless, the **C & M – B L A** can be seen as completely new version of outdated managers who were just task oriented. Moreover, this new approach is based on effective communication and motivation, which will improve people productivity, an essential thing in the world of modern business.

It is not the only style though. There is another leadership style which can be widely utilised by modern businesses in order to create highly responsive and competitive work environment. The new style of leadership can by described by words such as **Visionary Father – Leadership Approach**. The example of family can provide an extremely important image of a highly motivated and an effective group of people. In the case of good father, the future of his kids plays the most important role. Now, to provide kids with the best possible solutions which are essential to develop their capabilities, an effective cooperation is essential. Therefore, communication and motivation are the most important components which have to be explored in order to create an image for an optimistic future. To inspire your kids, it is essential to have interesting personality, the personality which is full of understanding, trust and love.

If modern leadership will be able to understand that the family environment in some cases is similar to the business environment, and the creation of common future will not be all that difficult to form. Are things the same if we make the workplace a new setting? A new workplace or any different business environment comprises of completely different personalities, and that makes it challenging to create strong and reliable business conditions. Till there is not a way to develop or put into practice the **Visionary Father – Leadership Approach**, we can use **C & M – B L A**. It can be very useful to find the most effective ways of managing people. The goals concerned with the stable and responsive environments could be accomplished through the **C&M – BLA**. Once this step has been achieved, the next step will be converting to the Visionary Father – Leadership Approach.

The Visionary Father – Leadership Approach is the most effective method which can be used in order to create a future with trusted and highly knowledgeable people who are not only the right people for the right job but also passionate about their jobs. It is so important to have people who outperform not because of the money factor but because of the culture they represent. Such goal-setting will provide ground-breaking results for the organisation if such an approach is implemented successful in their leadership bloodlines.

Let's take an example of the household again. So, if the household does not have equality, will the head of the family be treated with the same respect? Yes, in most cases as the head would be using his autocratic power to assert his law onto his dependents. Will that acceptance from the family members be willing? Of course not. What if the father treats all his sons and daughters equally? What if he distributes the rewards evenly without any discrimination and motivates them to remain a team. Will that culture be different? Surely, it would be a much joyful and stress-free environment to operate in than the one before.

So, just like this father and the rest of the family, any business, organisation, government carries with it the same concept: The concept of a family. Hence, this concept needs to adopted for a smooth process. Failing to adopt this into action and staying with that autocratic father would bring in the results but not quality and motivation.

All the motivational and leadership dilemmas we have brought light onto, they all lack the father approach. What does that mean? It means that leadership is already there in the market but it is not the right type of leadership. The right form of leadership is the **Visionary Father – Leadership Approach**.

This approach can be hard to implement as different organisations have different cultures but if done efficiently, it will take those organisations to levels they cannot imagine now. Such is the power of coordinated efforts than pressured goals. There has been a lot of research over time on what motivates employees and how that can help bring in more productivity, but this approach solely can bring in all those elements of motivation and other vital components of leadership together.

The biggest factor that can greatly contribute to this new leadership style is the adoption of this approach. To do this effectively, researches and experiments would have to be carried out in the organisations in order to understand all the different cultures of leadership personalities. But once done, this customised approach will be used to make sure the parts assigned to each member in the team are performed with quality and diligence.

Autocratic leadership will stay but it needs to be readjusted to specific power organisations which readily rely on regulation. For organisations involved in creativity, teamwork and the overall business, Democratic leadership is the key to success in the modern leadership. This Democratic Leadership can only be achieved if the concept of **Visionary Father – Leadership Approach** is applied within it. The reason for that is pretty simple. This style has been existent with the Autocratic approach but has always been used in autocratic ways, creating deceptive ways to showcase the real Democratic Leadership.

Just like any country which proclaims it is Democratic, it is not always the case. Likewise, Democratic Leadership is not Democratic until it utilises the core concepts such as the ones we have mentioned in all the chapters. But most importantly, the approach of **Visionary Father Leadership** is the founding stone of Democratic Leadership Style. In order to make Democratic Leadership successful, all these notions will have to be applied and implemented within the organisations.

With such a fast change in the business environment, leadership too is asking for a change. It is no longer the time when one person will have the power over others. Companies are using mini-CEOs and leaders in each department and creating amazing results for their business portfolios. It is time to act and become agile. This leadership is the new future and if companies try to stay away from this endorsement, they will be the same as Nokia in some years.

Trends in the markets are no longer centralised and even the governmental institutions are privatising their units. This sole justification shows the reasons to have modern leadership implemented for any business. This adaptation of modern leadership will not only provide a head-start to the company, but will strengthen its position in the market, both in its shares and growth. The time to act is Now. Leadership is no longer simple. One has to craft it by using the proper models and approaches in order for it work effectively. The modern times cannot run an outdated version of leadership. It is time to run Modern Times with Modern Leadership.

NOTES

NOTES

NOTES

NOTES

REFERENCES

Apple Press Info (2016) [online] available from <http://www.apple.com/pr/library/2015/10/27Apple-Reports-Record-Fourth-Quarter-Results.html> (25.01.2016)

About education (2015) Kurt Lewin Biography (1890-1947) [online] available from <http://psychology.about.com/od/profilesofmajorthinkers/p/bio_lewin.htm> (23.10.2015)

Allegheny College (2015) 12 Strategies for Motivation That Work [online] available from <http://sites.allegheny.edu/deanofstudents/wellness-education/todays-topic/12-strategies-for-motivation-that-work/> (13.01.2016)

An Empirical Study of Leadership Styles Journal of Economic Development, Management, IT, Finance and Marketing 5 (2) 1-31

Adaptive Leaders Ship Style [online] available from <http://www.forbes.com/sites/travisbradberry/2012/11/09/leadership-2-0-are-you-an-adaptive-leader/> (25.11.2015)

Bass, B. M. (1985) Leadership and performance beyond expectations. New York, NY: Free Press

Basu, R., Green, S, G. (1997) 'Leader–member exchange and transformational leadership: An empirical examination of innovative behaviours in leader–member dyads' Journal of Applied Social Psychology 27 (6) 477–499

Business News Daily (2015) What Kind of Leader Are You? Traits, Skills and Styles [online] available from <http://www.businessnewsdaily.com/2704-leadership.html> (19.10.2015)

Business Case Studies (2015) The importance of effective management [online] available from <http://businesscasestudies.co.uk/cmi/the-importance-of-effective-management/leadership-and-management.html#axzz3pNsjmAU3> (23.10.2015)

Boykins, C., Campbell, S., Moore and M,. Nayyar, S. (2013) 'An Empirical Study of Leadership Styles 5' Journal of Economic Development, Management, IT, Finance and Marketing 1 (2) 1-31

Boyle, D. M., Mahoney, D. P., Carpenter, B. W., and Grambo, R. J. (2014) 'The Importance of Communication Skills at Different Career Levels: Management'. Career Paths 84 (8) 40-45

Baesu, C., Bejinaru R (2015) 'Innovative Leadership Styles and The Influence of Emotional Intelligence' USV Annals of Economics & Public Administration 15 (10) 136-145

Bar-On, R. (1997) The emotional quotient inventory (EQ-i): a test of emotional intelligence. Toronto: Multi-Health Systems

Baker, H. K. & Nofsinger, J. R. (2012) Socially Responsible Finance and Investing. US: Wiley, Somerset

Benincasa, R. (2012). 6 Leadership Styles, And When You Should Use Them [online] available from <http://www.fastcompany.com/1838481/6-leadership-styles-and-when-you-shoulduse-them> (28.10.2015). cited in Cameron Boykins, Scott Campbell, Michelle Moore, Shikha Nayyar (2013) 'An Empirical Study of Leadership Styles' Journal of Economic Development, Management, IT, Finance and Marketing 5 (2) 1-31

Benincasa, R. (2012). 6 Leadership Styles, And When You Should Use Them [online] available from <http://www.fastcompany.com/1838481/6-leadership-styles-and-when-you-shoulduse-them> (28.10.2015) Cited in Cameron Boykins, Scott Campbell, Michelle Moore, Shikha Nayyar (2013)

Bell, J. (2005) Doing your Research Project. Buckingham: Open University Press

Brands, R. (2010) 'Innovation Made Incarnate' Employee Motivation, Success in Business, Innovations in Business 2 (2) 1

Business Insider (2015) How Facebook Managed 3,000 Twenty-Somethings Into A $100 Billion Company [online] available from <http://www.businessinsider.com/facebooks-100-billion-management-secrets-2012-3?IR=T> (09.02.2015)

Crush, F. P., Jeffery J, Kirton, R., Lewis, H., Scott, G., Waller, A. D. 'Recruit Better with strengths based interviewing' People Management 34-34

Comparative features of the transactional and transformational leadership [online] available from <http://leadingengineers.org/category/transformational-leadership/> (25.11.2015)

Chron (2015) Theories on Motivation in Organizations and Management [online] available from <http://smallbusiness.chron.com/theories-motivation-organizations-management-25221.html> (19.10.2015)

Business Insider (2015) How Facebook Managed 3,000 Twenty-Somethings Into A $100 Billion Company [online] available from <http://www.businessinsider.com/facebooks-100-billion-management-secrets-2012-3?IR=T> (09.02.2015)

Crush, F, P,. Jeffery J, Kirton, R,. Lewis, H,. Scott, G,. Waller, A, D. 'Recruit Better with strengths based interviewing' People Management 34-34

Comparative features of the transactional and transformational leadership [online] available from <http://leadingengineers.org/category/transformational-leadership/> (25.11.2015)

Chron (2015) Theories on Motivation in Organizations and Management [online] available from <http://smallbusiness.chron.com/theories-motivation-organizations-management-25221.html> (19.10.2015)

Chron (2016) Importance of Effective Recoupment &Selection [online] available from <http://smallbusiness.chron.com/importance-effective-recruitment-selection-55782.html> (12.01.2016)

Chief Executive (2015) The 2015 best companies for leadership [online] available from < http://chiefexecutive.net/2015-best-companies-leaders/#prettyPhoto> (04.01.2016)

Chief Executive (2015) The most effectively managed companies in terms of leadership [online] available from <http://chiefexecutive.net/2015-best-companies-leaders/> (25.11.2015)

Fraser S, P (2015) 'Transformative Science Teaching in Higher Education' Journal of Transformational Education 13 (2) 140-160

Forbes (2015) The World's Most Valuable Brands [online] available online <http://www.forbes.com/powerful-brands/list/ > (20.10.2015)

Forbes (2015) Where Are You on a Hierarchy of Investor Needs [online] available from <http://www.forbes.com/sites/financialfinesse/2015/07/15/where-are-you-on-the-hierarchy-of-investment-needs/#2d470c6b4788412234144788> (13.01.2016)

Forbes (2015) Five reasons 8 Out OF 10 Businesses Fail [online] available from http://www.forbes.com/sites/ericwagner/2013/09/12/five-reasons-8-out-of-10-businesses-fail/ (29.01.2016)

Forbes (2015) The World's Most Valuable Brands [online] available online <http://www.forbes.com/powerful-brands/list/ > (20.10.2015)

Forbes (2015) Where Are You on a Hierarchy of Investor Needs [online] available from <http://www.forbes.com/sites/financialfinesse/2015/07/15/where-are-you-on-the-hierarchy-of-investment-needs/#2d470c6b4788412234144788> (13.01.2016)

Forbes (2015) Five reasons 8 Out OF 10 Businesses Fail [online] available from http://www.forbes.com/sites/ericwagner/2013/09/12/five-reasons-8-out-of-10-businesses-fail/ (29.01.2016)

Forbes (2012) Leadership 2.0: Are You An Adaptive Leader? [online] available from <http://www.forbes.com/sites/travisbradberry/2012/11/09/leadership-2-0-are-you-an-adaptive-leader/#300d24f17d81> (18.03.2016)

Ghasabeh, M, S,. Soosay, C. and Reaiche, C. (2015) 'The Emerging Role of Transformational Leadership' The Journal of Developing Areas 49 (6) 460-464

Goddard, W., Melville, S. (2004) Research Methodology: An Introduction. 2nd edition, Blackwell Publishing

Hierarchical Taxonomy of Leadership stales [online] available from <http://search.ebscohost.com/login.aspx?direct=true&db=bth&AN=84930149&site=bsi-live> (25.11.2015)

Independent (2015) A quarter of UK professionals are unhappy with their work-life balance, survey finds [online] available from <http://www.independent.co.uk/news/business/news/a-quarter-of-uk-professionals-are-unhappy-with-their-work-life-balance-survey-finds-10071994.html> (22.10.2015)

Johnson, G,. Whittington, R., Scholes, K,. Angwin, D,. Regner, P. (2014) Exploring Strategy. Edinburgh Gate: Person Education Limited

Kendra Cherry (2010) 'Lewin's Leadership Styles' Executive Leadership 26 (10) 1-3

Lewin, A. and Minton, J (1986) 'Determining Organisational Effectiveness: Another look, and an agenda for research' Management science 32 (5) 514

Livermore, D. (2013) 'How Facebook Develops Its Global Leaders David Livermore, in a conversation with Bill McLawtion at Facebook' People & Strategy 36 (3) 24-25

Leadership-central.com (2015) Types of Motivation [online] available from <http://www.leadership-central.com/types-of-motivation.html#axzz3yLROGAZB> (26.01.2015) Management of Apple Inc. (2015) Motivation [online] available from <https://managementofapple.wordpress.com/motivation/> (09.03.2016)

Mayol, F. C., Ramesh, F. S., Quarterl, M. 'New research suggests that the secret to developing effective leaders is to encourage four types of behaviour.'
Business Source Complete 4 (4) 88-91

MindTools (2013). Leadership Styles Leadership Skills [online] available from <http://www.mindtools.com/pages/article/newLDR_84.htm>(29.10.2015) Cited in Cameron Boykins, McDermott. , Aoife M., Conway. Edel. Rousseau. , Denise M., Flood. Patrick C (2013) Promoting Effective Psychological Contracts Through Leadership: The Missing Link Between HR Strategy and Performance 'Human Resource Management 52 (2) 289-310

Morley, M. (2013) Task vs. Relationship Leadership Theories [online] available from < http://smallbusiness.chron.com/task-vs-relationshipleadership-theories-35167.html> (28.10. 2015). Cited in Cameron Boykins, Scott Campbell, Michelle Moore, Shikha Nayyar (2013) Journal of Economic Development, Management, IT, Finance and Marketing: An Empirical Study of Leadership Styles' 5 (2) 1-31

Meyer, S. (2012). Five Leadership Styles for Successful Project Management [online] available from <http://leadonpurposeblog.com/2012/10/20/five-leadership-styles-for-successfulproject-management/> (28.10.2015). Cited in Cameron Boykins, Scott Campbell, Michelle Moore, Shikha Nayyar (2013) Journal of Economic Development, Management, IT, Finance and Marketing: An Empirical Study of Leadership Styles' 5 (2), 1-31

Mihai J, P, A, Sorin, D. (2010) 'Using Lean Six Sigma as a Motivational Tool for Processes Improvement.' Annals of the University of Oradea, Economic Science Series 19 (2) 438 – 442

Meyer, S. (2012). Five Leadership Styles for Successful Project Management [online] available from <http://leadonpurposeblog.com/2012/10/20/five-leadership-styles-for-successfulproject-management/> (28.10.2015). Cited in Cameron Boykins, Scott Campbell, Michelle Moore, Shikha Nayyar (2013) Journal of Economic Development, Management, IT, Finance and Marketing: An Empirical Study of Leadership Styles' 5 (2), 1-31

Mihai J, P, A, Sorin, D. (2010) 'Using Lean Six Sigma as a Motivational Tool for Processes Improvement.' Annals of the University of Oradea, Economic Science Series 19 (2) 438 – 442

Maslow's Hierarchy of Needs [online] available from <https://www.boundless.com/management/textbooks/boundless-management-textbook/organizational-behavior-5/employee-needs-and-motivation-46/maslow-s-hierarchy-of-needs-171-7621/> (18.03.2016)

Nokia (2016) Our company [online] available from <http://company.nokia.com/en/about-us/our-company/our-story> (08.02.2016)

Nokia Q1 2013 results - slow but steady improvements [online] available from <http://allaboutwindowsphone.com/news/item/17321_nokia_q1_2013_results-slow_but.php> (18.03.2016)

Palmer, B. and Stough, C. (2001) 'Swinburne University Emotional Intelligence Test. Interim Technical Manual' Organisational Psychology Research 2 (2) 3-11

Parliamentary and Health Service Ombudsman (2015) Only one in three people complain to a public service when they are unhappy, according to new research [online] available from <http://www.ombudsman.org.uk/about-us/news-centre/press-releases/2015/only-one-in-three-people-complain-to-a-public-service-when-they-are-unhappy,-according-to-new-research>(21.10.2016)

Remenyi, D., Williams, B., Money, A., Swartz, E. (1998) Doing Research in Business and Management: An introduction To process and method. London: Sage

Suan S, C, T, Anantharaman, R, N. and Tong Yoon Kin, D. (2015) Essential factors necessary to create effective organisational performance. 'Emotional Intelligence' and Organisational Performance.' Global Business and Management Research: An International Journal 7 (2) 37-43

Suan S, C, T, Anantharaman, R, N. and Tong Yoon Kin, D. (2015) Essential factors necessary to create effective organisational performance. 'Emotional Intelligence' and Organisational Performance.' Global Business and Management Research: An International Journal 7 (2) 37-43

Scott Campbell, Michelle Moore, Shikha Nayyar (2013) 'An Empirical Study of Leadership Styles' Journal of Economic Development, Management, IT, Finance and Marketing 5 (2) 1-31

Suan S, C, T., Anantharaman, R, N., Tong Yoon Kin, D. (2015) 'Emotional Intelligence' and Organisational Performance.' Global Business and Management Research: An International Journal (2) 37-43

Simons, M. and Ridder, J. (2004) 'Renewing Connections and Changing Relations' Use of Information and Communication Technology and Cohesion in Organizational Groups Communications 29 (2)

Saunders, M., Lewis, P., Thornhill, A. (2009) Research methods for business students. Harlow: Person Education

SHAGANAA (2014) APPLE'S INTERNAL COMMUNICATIONS STRATEGY [online] available form <https://shaganaas.wordpress.com/2014/05/02/apples-internal-communications-strategy/> (09.03.2016)

Smith, E, M. Thorpe, R., Jackson, P. and Lowe, A. (2008) Management Research. London: Sage

Travis, E. (2013). What Is Hands-On Leadership [online available from]
< http://smallbusiness.chron.com/handson-leadership-24933.html> (28.10.2015). Cited in Cameron Boykins, Scott Campbell, Michelle Moore, Shikha Nayyar (2013) Journal of Economic Development, Management, IT, Finance and Marketing: An Empirical Study of Leadership Styles' 5 (2) 1-31

Transactional vs Transformational Leadership [online] available from
< http://www.slideshare.net/IssaGo/transactional-vs-transformational-leadership> (18.03.2016)

UK Essays (2015) Research Onion | Explanation of the Concept [online] available from <http://www.ukessays.com/essays/psychology/explanation-of-the-concept-of-research-onion-psychology-essay.php> (09.02.2016)

University of Kent (2016) Strengths-Based Interview [online] available from <http://www.kent.ac.uk/careers/interviews/strength-based-interviews.htm> (12.01.2016)

Yukl, G. (2012) 'Effective Leadership Behaviour: What We Know and What Questions Need More Attention' Academy of Management Perspectives 26 (4) 66-85

Yue, Z., Syed, A. (2014) 'How transformational leadership influences follower helping behaviour: The role of trust and prosocial motivation' Journal or Organizational Behaviour 35 (3) 373-392

Yin, R.K. (2014) Case Study Research. Design and Method. London:

Meet Thomas Gralak

My name is Thomas John Gralak. I was born in Poland in the year, 1983. The beginning of my young life started in the midst of the communist Poland. It was a very short but strong to the memory period. It was also the time when I witnessed genuine happiness because of the way people were communicating with me, and I would regard it as surreal and majestic moment of truth in my life.

Like many families, we too were going through a hard time. Some family issues I'm mentioned in the book irrevocably changed my life, and I was in a very difficult situation, very near to going homeless. Drug addiction, alcohol, and internal pain were causing my life colossal damage, both physically and mentally. But then I won the brown and silver medals at the Polish Boxing Championship.

I stepped back in life to reflect and then started my life from ground zero. The passion of sport and training people provided me an aim for my newly-found life. These new experiences gave me the courage to start my academic excursions at Coventry University in England. This time in my life gave me the possibility to experience some of the best education in the world, and also made it possible for me to meet enthralling characters, people who have changed the way I see the world now.

During my studies in England, I decided to start my carrier as a lecturer and a trainer because of my yearning love for communication. I started to understand how communication worked and how deeply it influences our life. The plethora of knowledge did not let my brain stay away from writing about it. So, I decided to share the knowledge which had saved my life. I wanted to treat people the same way I was treated by the sagas who revamped my life for the better and forever.

For many years, I have been working as a lecturer at Polish universities. Along with my teaching powers, I run my own company called TG Training where I try to promote and enlighten my students about the real spirit of communication; the real communication.

Other Books by Thomas Gralak

ARE YOU REALLY COMMUNICATING?

www.ingramcontent.com/pod-product-compliance
Lightning Source LLC
Chambersburg PA
CBHW070442220526
45466CB00004B/1756